HOW TO MAKE THE
"SHIPS" WORK

MARQUES D. NEAL

By: **Marques D. Neal**

Created by: Jabez Publishing House

Designed by: J.Michael Advertising

Copyright Disclaimer

Biblical Reference

Unless otherwise noted, scripture reference taken from the King James Version of the Bible.

New International Version. [Colorado Springs]: Biblica, 2011. BibleGateway.com. Web. 3 Mar. 2011.

Scripture quotations taken from the New American Standard Bible®,Copyright © 1960, 1962, 1963, 1968, 1971, 1972, 1973, 1975, 1977, 1995 by The Lockman Foundation Used by permission." (www.Lockman.org)

Scripture quotations taken from the Amplified® Bible, Copyright © 1954, 1958, 1962, 1964, 1965, 1987 by The Lockman Foundation Used by permission. (www.Lockman.org)

Acknowledgements

First and foremost, I want to say "Thank You" and give all praise to my Lord and Savior Jesus Christ for being a Keeper, a Provider, a Friend, and a Lover...getting me through every tough time of my life.

To my best friend, my covenant partner and soul mate, Lady Lisa Neal, who has been my rock and who encourages and inspires me to be all that I can be and to go after everything God has for me. You are truly a gift from God.

To my children ~Donovan, Michael, Princess, Marques II, Sidney II and Jeremiah. I cannot find the words to say how much you all mean to me. You are my joy and motivation, and my heart. I believe in you and I'm so proud of you.

Your future is so bright.

To Lion of Judah "The Family Center"...You guys are the best. I'm so thankful for the hard work and all you do to help make Judah successful, and all your support you give me as your Pastor. Your fuel is the fire that drives me to reach the world with the Gospel of Jesus Christ.

~ Marques D. Neal ~

TABLE OF CONTENTS

Foreword

Be driven and inspired by this revelatory work that brings together most, if not all, of the dynamics to make "ships" work. Marques Neal not only takes his personal journey to add cement to the bonding required for relationships, but he also adds in the spiritual matter to effect long-lasting friendships. It is the process of viewing the experiences of life, the challenges and detours that make us strong, and coating these with our relationship with Christ, that leads us to learn about our self "ship" and what it takes to meld us into relationships and friendships. This blending and combining becomes an intimate work that may take a little time for some, and for most of us-- for the "ships" to be truly cemented--takes a lifetime.

As you read this book, tune in to the modestly majestic way that we are taught through three points and many steps of wisdom as the man himself teaches us: "Spend time with those that time is worth spending with ~ wasted time can never be gotten back!"

Let's get delivered and get our ships in order. It's all about the ships….got yours?

INTRODUCTION

Knowing What It Takes
To Make Your Journey Successful

I am a firm believer that, as the scripture says in Hosea 4:6, "People are destroyed for the lack of knowledge."

Destroyed ~ to be completely ruined, spoiled, or killed

Lack ~ to be in need of something

Knowledge ~ to have awareness, understanding and information

Success will always be challenging for you if you are:

1. Unsure of who you are

2. Trying to accomplish something without the necessary components

3. Ignorant to your surroundings

I decided to write this book out of my personal experience and my awareness of how people struggle, get stuck, and waste years of their lives due to bad decision-making in the most important areas of their lives.

Marques D. Neal

PART I

Friendship

CHAPTER 1

Proper Preparation

This has become a generation that wants everything quick, fast, and in a hurry, and will not take the time to do their homework. Remember this: investigation will always result in elevation. The more you know, the greater your chances are for being successful. I have always heard the saying that life is like a box of chocolates: you never know what you're going to get. Well, I have never gone to the store and gotten me a box of chocolates that did not have three things:

1. A container to hold the chocolates
2. A label to let me know what kind of chocolates are in the box
3. An expiration date to let me know how long the

chocolates will last

So, I knew exactly what I was getting, and I would stand there and choose exactly what I wanted—what I knew would satisfy me.

To help you to have a successful journey you must look for three things:

1. The person's container:

   How do they keep themselves up, because if they can't keep themselves up how will they be able to keep you?

2. Their label:

   When talking to the person, what does it tell you about them? How much has been invested in them? What ingredients were used to help make them who they are?

3. Their expiration date:

   Ask yourself, if I did this based off of the information this is giving me, how long will this really last? What are my chances of getting exactly what I want, and will it satisfy me to the fullest?

I do agree that in one way life *is* like a box of chocolates. It can be very enjoyable. But, not knowing what you will get? This is not so true. Not if you just take the time to stop, pick up the box, read the label, and pay attention to the signs of what it is that you want, instead of just grabbing the first thing you walk by and throwing it in the cart because you are in such a hurry. If you don't pay attention, you find you've paid for an impulse purchase, only to get home and realize that you've ended up with something you don't want. There are some things that, once you've opened them and trying them out, cannot be so easily returned.

I wanted to give people something to hold on to: something like a guideline. Here are some helpful tools to look at that would help make your decision-making process just a little easier— something that could take a load off your mind, because if you knew better, then hopefully you would strive to *do* better.

I lost my virginity at the age of 12, preached my first sermon at the age of 15, was ordained an Elder at the age of 17, had my first child at the age of 18, married and had a second child on the way at the age of 22, and started Lion Of Judah TFC at the age of 25. Through these life-altering transitions, I had to grow and mature very fast. So I had to learn how to make the ships work, because my life and destination depended on it. One of the greatest things that helped me develop in a mighty way was getting around people who were full of wisdom that they could impart in to me.

Because of my trials and tests and lessons learned, I strongly feel that I can be a help to many people in getting through some difficult times, and help others to avoid them. This book just might be what you need. Ships are made to help us get from one place to another. If you are on a ship that's not taking you where you need to go, you might want to consider getting off.

S.H.I.P

SACRIFICING - HONEST - INVOLVED - PEOPLE

CHAPTER 2

Friendship

50/50 Keeping It Balanced

Loneliness is everywhere. Many people feel cut off and alienated (*"to make indifferent or hostile; to turn away, transfer or divert"*) from others. Being in a crowd only makes people more aware of their isolation (*"to set or place apart; to detach or separate, as to be along; the complete separation from others; as of a person suffering from a contagious or infectious disease; quarantine"*). We all need friends who will stick close, listen, care, and offer help when it is needed—in good times as well as bad. It is better to have one such friend than dozens of superficial acquaintances (*"a person known to one but usually not a close friend; personal knowledge as a result of study or experience"*). Instead of wishing you could find a true friend, seek to become one. There are people who need your friendship. Ask God to reveal them to you, and then take on the challenge of being a true friend.

> **Friend** - a person who gives assistance; patron; supporter; A person who is on good terms with another; a person who is not hostile (*"opposed in feelings or non-hospitable; not friendly"*)

Plato's Cave

Plato, a famous Greek philosopher, had a theory about how people fool themselves. He tried explaining his theory to others by telling this story:

> Some people were living inside a cave that had an opening to allow sunlight to enter. These people were chained to the ground, so that none of them could ever leave the cave. As the sun moved throughout the day, so did the shadows of things outside the cave. The people thought that the shadows were in fact living things, and that the sounds they heard through that same opening were the voices of the shadows.

Get Out of Your Cave

How many times have you gone out of your way to avoid the truth, and done everything in your power to fool yourself that it's really not that way. The people in Plato's Cave were living in their own imaginary world, perceiving things very differently from the true nature of things, and so they continued to live with false beliefs. How often do you confine yourself to the four walls of your house, or within the entrapment of your mind, just like these people who had a glimpse of hope? That glimpse of hope was the sunlight that provided shadows that were an indication of other humans just outside the cave. This was a call for help, but, because they were stuck in their own world, they continued to believe that the shadows were alive and indeed were the ones doing the talking. Because of this, they believed that the shadows were insignificant, that the shadows could do nothing to help them. Never get to the place in life where you make shadow people real people. Don't chain yourself to your own issues and previous encounters. Who knows, the people in Plato's Cave could have been one cry away from freedom. If they just could have seen the truth. When you are able to accept the truth and see what's real, a cry for help will never be hard, and if you have a true friend they will be willing to do whatever it takes to rescue you from your cave. A lot of people live their lives thinking that they are boring or ugly, and this makes them misunderstand every message they get from others, and these misunderstandings serve as further proof of their false beliefs. If you can't imagine how this can occur, then take a look at these examples:

They hate me:

Do you sometimes feel that people dislike you even though you don't have any proof to support your feelings?

They were bored with me:

Do you sometimes misinterpret any move, smile, or tiny action from another person and then go home thinking you left a bad impression?

They aren't enjoying my company:

Do you sometimes get back home feeling sad because you felt that people weren't enjoying your company even though you actually have no real evidence to prove this?

The PROBLEM WITH SELF-DECEPTION

Self-deception is the fastest way to lose someone. This happens when you incorrectly interpret a small action made by someone and believe that action means they don't like you. This can ruin your friendship with that person. Without even noticing, you will most likely start to avoid that person, and may even wait for the slightest mistake they make to pick a fight. If they notice the aloof or hostile attitude you have towards them, they may start to treat you the same way and this provides you with even more "proof" of your false belief. You will end up being convinced one-hundred percent that they hate you. Now you have just lost the friendship of a person who didn't have any bad intentions towards you. Self-deception can lead to destroying your friendship with your partner, work mate, boss, and anyone else you care for.

Lack of Understanding and Friendship Dissatisfaction

Lack of understanding of your friends' needs and wants can lead to friendship dissatisfaction. Lack of self-understanding and lack of understanding of your friends' emotions can be the main reason behind break-ups and loss of friendships. It's important that you try not to have fights with your friend. It's important not to complain before you make sure that you have the facts right, or else you will be risking your friendship. Every healthy and successful friendship is based on understanding the importance of it being 50/50, and maintaining that healthy balance. There are two steps you can take to prevent self-deception from happening.

1. Challenge Your Thoughts

   If someone doesn't call you, don't jump to the conclusion that they no longer want to be bothered with you. Instead try to think of a reasonable explanation for why they didn't call. Unless you have some really strong evidence, then you probably are wrong.

2. Build Self Confidence

   Since the main reason for incorrect perceptions is that you are not feeling confident enough about yourself, building self-confidence can help you solve this problem. If you were self-confident, you would have thought of any other explanation for your friend's behavior rather than believing that they just may not like you. Don't live in Plato's Cave. Break your chains and explore the world outside. You will see that it has so much more to offer than what you have become accustomed to.

CHAPTER 3

Knowing How to Have
a Lasting Friendship

Do you have a good friend? Do you make friends easily, or is it hard work for you? Proverbs 18:24 (revised) tells us, "A man who has friends must himself be friendly." You will only get what you are willing to put out. How you extend yourself will be how you are received. Sometimes your actions and how you are perceived is as a "chaser" rather than a "drawer". No one wants to be around a person who is not pleasant, caring, and understanding. If you always come off like you are on the defensive about something, you will miss out on having some good people in your life. I have collected 35 tips for you on knowing how to have a lasting friendship. Some of the tips are about finding friends, and others are about how to deepen a friendship once it's formed. Finally, I offer some points on how to repair a friendship.

A friend recently said to me: "What if I were to be convicted of a crime, even if I were innocent, and got put in jail for ten years. Who will be at the gates when I'm released?" This is a powerful question and a great test of any friendship. Let's take a closer look at it.

1. Your friend is charged with a crime that they say they did not do:

    This becomes a matter of how well you know your friend, and whether you believe they are capable of committing the crime they are accused of. Is the friendship strong enough for you to stand by it? It's so easy to stand by someone when all is well and everything is going good, but true friendship is proven in the worst of times.

2. To get ten years of jail time:

    How many times in that ten years would you go and visit? Would you do everything possible to find a way to get them out? Would they be able to depend on your assistance?

3. And who *would* be at the gate:

> While your friend is going through the process of being
> released, would it be going through their mind that they
> really don't know if anyone is out there waiting on
> them, or do they know for sure, without a doubt, that
> you are at that gate?

Could you rely on some of your friends to be there if that
happened to you? What is your definition of a friend?

It's common to feel lonely, to think of yourself as something
small and solitary in the vastness of things. It's easy, then, to
think of a friend as a home territory, carved out of that vastness.
A friend can be a kind of living diary for sharing and storing the
feelings of the day so that life can go on more or less as usual.
Yet, there are other kinds of friendships that don't simply
assuage loneliness but actually dispel it by changing your
understanding of who you are. Good friends help us understand
who we really are.

To create and enjoy lasting friends takes effort and skill. Some
people make friends easily, but for many of us making and
keeping friends isn't always easy. Here is a list of ways to create
and cultivate lasting friends:

First and foremost, know yourself. In order to make friends we need to know who we are. If you are not clear on what your life's purpose is, you may be a hindrance to someone else achieving theirs.

A – Personality

What is your personality? Take a look at the following. Are you?

An idealistic reformer

A caring helper

A success-oriented achiever

An introspective idealist

A sensitive individualist

An intense investigator

A security-oriented loyalist

A spontaneous enthusiast

A powerful challenger

A reassuring peace maker

B – Signature Style

What is your signature style? Are you engaging, entertaining, moving, intense, funny, bold, ditzy, serene, boring, or threatening?

C – Beliefs

What do you believe about life, the universe, or about yourself? Do you have religious beliefs? Do you have beliefs about yourself that limit your potential?

D – Spirituality

Are you drawn to the mysteries of life? Do you use spiritual practice? i.e. meditation, prayer or other practices to nurture your spirituality?

E – Aspirations

What are your aspirations? Do you strive for a cause that is greater than you?

F – Thoughts

What kind of thoughts are mostly in your mind? Are they daydreams, or thoughts focused on your current project? Is your mind usually focused on the past, on the present, or on the future?

G – Goals

What are your goals? Have you recorded them? The habit of goal-setting, and which goals we choose determines a substantial part of our uniqueness.

H – Creativity

Are you creative? Do you create at work, or write, paint, cook, or in any other way are you creative? Often, people who are creative are more lively and happy than those who are not.

I – Happiness

How happy are you?

J – Attitude

What is your habitual attitude? Is it negative or positive? Our attitude is shaped by the influences of our associations, beliefs, thoughts, expectations, and self-talk. How has your attitude been shaped?

K – Attraction

What are you drawn to? What are your favorite colors? What's your favorite music, climate, or food? What kind of people do you like?

L – Face

The face is a mirror of the soul. If we are kind and upbeat, our face looks animated and relaxed. If we feel down or anxious or ill, our face looks tight and grey. What is your face like? Do you take moments to relax your face?

M – Voice

We are born with a particular voice, with its own resonance, tone and pitch. However, it can be developed, as actors and singers do. Know what your unique voice is like.

N – Diction

Definition – Style of speaking or writing as dependent upon choice of words; the accent, inflection, intonation, and speech-sound quality manifested by an individual speaker usually judged in terms of prevailing standards of acceptability; enunciation. Do you speak with an accent or a dialect? The way we pronounce the language we use is a unique marker.

O – Hormones

Hormonal patterns determine whether we are tired or hungry or irritated or lustful. What hormonal patterns or surges are noticeable in your life, and how do they influence you?

P – Age

Age is a biological factor. But, it is also influenced by the mind. Do you feel old and unfit, low on energy and drive? Or, do you feel vitally alive, energetic, and youthful? If you want to feel youthful, you need to put effort into keeping your mind and body in good shape. How do you keep in good shape?

Q – Intelligence

Being intelligent is not only having a high IQ. Intelligence is now seen to include social, emotional, and physical factors, and the mixture of these strands of intelligence is what makes you unique. How do you maintain and develop your intelligence?

R – Life Experience

Each of us has a unique experience of life. Used wisely, experience is valuable, because we can recognize patterns and respond appropriately. Which life experience has shaped you the most?

S – Childhood

The childhood we experienced in the past makes us unique today. What was your childhood like? How has it shaped you? If your childhood included traumatic experiences, what have you undertaken in order to heal from this?

T – Trauma

What kind of life crises have you experienced? Have you integrated these, or are they still unresolved? You must learn how to turn tragedy into triumph, and know that you can win.

U – Opportunities

We have all encountered different opportunities in life. What kinds of opportunities have you encountered or dreaded? How have you responded to these? What we make of opportunities is partly what makes us special.

V – Relationships

Who and what we relate to makes us who we are. Which human beings do you love or feel connected to? Who do you feel disconnected from? Coming out of a bad relationship, if not dealt with, can mess up a potentially good friendship, and having a good friendship can lead to a great relationship.

W – Habits

How do you spend your time on a regular basis? How much time do you spend on passive recreation such as TV? Do you have an unpaid activity that you enjoy? How important is this activity to you?

X – Work

Most people spend more time at work than asleep. How we spend this big chunk of our life makes us unique. What do you define as your main work? Do you work for yourself or work for others? Do you mostly work alone or with a team of people? Are you passionate about your work or is it a chore? Do you earn enough to keep yourself going or are you struggling financially?

Y – Communication Style

Psychologists pinpoint four different communication styles. Are you a: Relater, a Socializer, a Thinker, or a Director?

Z – The Life Journey

Each of us is on a unique life path. Which path we follow defines a path of our uniqueness. What path have your chosen?

What strikes me is that we are able to change most of these variables. What makes us truly special is how we spend our energy, thoughts, and time as well as how we respond to whom and what we encounter. It's in your power to evolve and bring forth the unique, special person that you are. That's an awesome responsibility. What do you realize about your life?

CHAPTER 4

Timeless Tools for Durability

Lasting – strong, durable, value and security

These words that describe "lasting" are so powerful. When making the "SHIP" work in a friendship, it is important to know this is so needed.

Strong – Does this friendship have what it takes to be able to handle the weight of whatever will come up during our time as friends?

Durable – Will it still be effective over a long period of time? Will it support the wear, tear, or decay that might happen as we go on throughout the years?

Value – How much does it really mean to you? How much work are you willing to put in? How far are you willing to go? How much is it worth to you?

Security – How much trust can be invested? Do you feel safe or comfortable sharing the most inner secret and private things in your life?

We take time to plan and format most aspects of our lives, but areas of friendships tend to be left to chance. At times, in the end, we neglect people who are sincere friends as they are shoved aside by daily routines, and then we awaken to our lack or despair. In some cases failure to evaluate friendships may result in much grief and pain. In the end, friendships are reciprocal; therefore, there should be some form of mutual enhancement of one another's well-being and good will.

Step 1

Study yourself and your value system, so that you may acquaint yourself with your inclinations before you start overloading your life with other people and their lives. This will give you a measured approach to friendship.

Step 2

Take time to love and respect yourself, and nurture yourself in a non-indulgent manner. Treating oneself with integrity is not selfish, but simply acknowledges a love and respect for oneself. This will help you choose friends who are honest, because untrustworthy friends can bring you undue trouble.

Step 3

Take practical steps to invest in yourself. This means studying who you are as an individual by listing your goals and ambitions, and setting out practical plans and schedules to fulfill your goals. Many people don't take time to develop and invest in themselves, and end up demanding too much from a friendship or engaging in trivial competitions and rivalries which will, in turn, destroy friendships.

Step 4

Choosing a friendship is an emotional investment. If you are to make such an investment, you need to take time to study the person carefully, in order to determine the type and nature of friendship that will work with a particular individual.

Step 5

Everyone is unique; therefore, friendships will vary in nature, but the key to successful friendships is having a sound knowledge of who *you* are, so that you don't lose your sense of self and your value system. As you interact with various people, review Step 3 often to make sure you are still in touch with yourself. Some dysfunctional friendships, or bitter endings to friendships, arise from an individual losing their individuality to someone else. The day that person walks out of their life, the one left behind falls apart. This may result in some people seeking to hurt the friend who is walking away.

Step 6

Maintain a healthy balance as you relate, taking care not to overly give, and then end up complaining that the friend is just a taker. Do not be addicted to receiving to the extent that the other person comes to perceive you as an emotional drainer, and end the friendship prematurely even if they may have been otherwise enjoying your friendship. Smothering friends with gifts, attention, excessive phone calls, endless suggestions, or excessive criticisms, may also have this emotional drain effect.

Step 7

Develop the ability to accept compliments without bragging, and the discipline to apologize and explain yourself whenever necessary, without evading the part of taking responsibility, and without blaming someone else.

Step 8

Allow each friendship to grow at its own pace. Develop

the areas of shared interest and be truthful to yourself and your friend, because lies bring distrust and destroy friendships quickly. Understand that you do not have to have a "one-friend-fits-all". You can have different friends for different activities, and allow each friendship to blossom at its own pace.

Step 9

Develop the discipline to confront a friend appropriately when necessary, and the discipline to forgive without licking wounds endlessly. If a friend deliberately causes you physical harm, or tries to harm you, then they are no longer a friend, and it's time to walk away. Friendship is a mutual enhancement of each other's well-being and good will.

CHAPTER 5

Tips & Warnings

✓ Don't rush friendships. Like a strong tree, let each friendship blossom at its own pace, so that it may be able to stand the sunny days as well as the rainy days.

✓ Telling a friend too much at one time can be overbearing.

✓ Choose your friends wisely, but most of all be a friend to yourself.

✓ Treat yourself with honor and integrity, and appreciate yourself and your daily living.

Just know that each season can bring new friendships, but that does not mean to destroy seasoned friendships.

Strong friendships can take years to build, and they're often the ones that last for a lifetime. A true friend is a confidant who will stand by you no matter what. If you want to develop a strong friendship with someone you have to be willing to make time for her/him, trust her/him, and be there for her/him. When she or he needs you, your nurturance can help them to become stronger.

Step 1 - Establish Trust

Be willing to share your private thoughts and feelings with your friend, and let the other person know that they can trust you with their feelings as well.

Step 2 – Laugh and Cry Together

Sharing an inside joke or a good cry bonds us to our friends.

Step 3 – Spend Time

Spend time with your friend even if your schedule is full and you don't have a lot of time. Meet for coffee or a quick lunch.

Step 4 – Acceptance of Flaws

Accept your friend's flaws. Overlook the little things that might annoy you about them, and love them for who they are.

Step 5 – Have Fun Together

More than likely you and your friends have shared interests and hobbies. Do these things together, and seek out new hobbies as well.

Step 6 – Express Your Feelings

Tell your friend how much they mean to you. If they are going through a rough period in their life send them a funny or encouraging card, drop off cookies or a box of chocolates. Or just stop by to see how they are doing.

Maintain a strong friendship. Though it may seem that friendships are merely nice to have, in truth they could actually help you live longer, according to an Australian study. Tom Veleo, writing for WebMD, reports that a Flinders University study found that people with an abundance of friends outlived those with markedly fewer friends. This means that putting effort into maintaining your current friendship will not just give you something to do on Saturday night, but also could tack some time onto your life.

Step 1 – Be Open

Friendships are all about openness and sharing. Though many people are reluctant to open themselves up to others for fear of being hurt, if you don't open yourself to your friends you will never form the kind of lasting bond that is necessary to maintain a friendship. Be trusting and allow your friends into your life completely, and allow them to have a life of their own. This will help keep your friendship on track. A strong friendship in some cases could actually be stronger than your own family:

I Samuel 20:16-42

Jonathan and David had a great bond and Jonathan loved David as he did his own self and Jonathan protected David his friend when he found out his father wanted to kill his friend.

Strong friends will always be willing to protect one another from harm, no matter what the cost is.

Step 2 – Support Each Other

Being there for each other through thick and thin is vital. If your friend needs your support, and you give them a shoulder to cry on or a sympathetic ear, they will reciprocate when you find yourself in need.

Hebrews 10:24-25

Says to let us consider one another in order to stir up love and good works, not forgetting to come together and exhort (lift up or support) each other.

Step 3 – Avoid Burying Issues

If you have long been friends with your closest chums, conflicts will certainly arise. To ensure that these conflicts don't become cancers that eat away at your friendship, deal with them instead of simply trying to push them aside. It is working through these kinds of issues this causes as little damage to friendships as possible.

Luke 17:3-4

"Be alert. If you see your friend going wrong, correct him. If he responds, forgive him. Even if it's personal against you and repeated seven times through the day, and seven times he says, I'm sorry, I won't do it again, forgive him."

Step 4 – Talk About It

Discuss problems with your friend directly. If you have a concern about your friend or are uncertain about something that pertains to your friendship, take this concern straight to your friend by speaking to them directly, instead of expressing your concern to others.

In this way, you can ensure that your friend doesn't feel as if you are talking about them behind their back.

Matthew 18:15-16

If a fellow believer hurts you go and tell him - work it out between the two of you. If he listens, you've made a friend. If he won't listen, take one or two others along so that the presence of witnesses will keep things honest, and try again.

Step 5 – Don't Smother Me

Avoid suffocation. While you may love your friend dearly, your friendship will likely suffer if you spend too much time together. To ensure that you don't get sick of each other take some alone time on occasion. This is often necessary when it comes to time with friends. There is such a thing as too much of a good thing.

Ecclesiastes 3:1 -
(There's a right time for everything)

There's an opportune time to do things, a right time for everything on the earth. Finding the right opportunity and perfect timing to do anything will always end up in having a fun and successful moment.

PART II

Relationships

CHAPTER 6

Your Choice Will Determine
Your Treatment

Choice – "the act of selecting; having the power, right, or freedom to choose".

One thing that needs to be noted is that just because you have freedom of choice, you should never be so quick to choose that you subject yourself to "settling." This is an important point to understand: freedom of choice gives you the power to pick what you want. *You* are the one doing the picking, so your selection is also your responsibility. You can never blame or point the finger at anyone for the choice that you decided to make, whether it turns out to be a good one or a bad one. You are always in control of this process of choosing. Be sure to make the best of it.

Treatment – "the act, manner, or method of handling or dealing with someone or something."

Treatment, Oh my God! Treatment! Treatment! Treatment! This can never be taken lightly. In any relationship this has to be #1 on the list and stay #1 on the list. It can never be compromised. Treatment will always let you know how the other person really feels about you. Their actions show you what you mean to them. Treatment flipped says how I meant to treat you. Remember the old saying that still stands true today: what you see is always what you will get. Don't be so foolish as to ignore what's clear, and subject yourself to treatment you don't deserve.

Relationships, perhaps more than any other facet of our lives, define who we are and what we value. Family ties, love, and relationships play a huge role in the overall happiness factor. So it stands to reason that establishing and maintaining healthy relationships should rank high on our list of priorities. Living in a healthy relationship can provide immense joy and personal satisfaction, but it can also be frustrating—as can everything good in life. A good relationship takes time and effort. Building healthy relationships is easy if you have the right tools. Knowing some basic tips for healthy relationships not only provides a basis for a strong relationship now but sets the stage for future relationships as well. This begins by recognizing the signs of a healthy relationship. It should be free of stress, mutually respectful, physically healthy and satisfying, and allow each party to maintain their individuality outside of the relationship. These 10 tips will help support you in your healthy relationship growth:

Realistic Expectations

This is true for any relationship, but it is particularly important when considering a romantic relationship. You may have found your Prince Charming but no one can be everything we might want him or her to be. Sometimes people disappoint, and this has to be taken into consideration. However, don't allow disappointment to become a habit. This can be avoided by not setting your expectations outrageously high.

Talk With Each Other

It can't be said enough that communication is essential in healthy relationships. It means taking the time to really, genuinely be there. Really listen, and don't just think about what you will say next while you should be listening. Don't interrupt, and listen not just with your ears but also with your heart.

Be Flexible

Most of us try to keep people and situations just the way we like them to be. It's natural to feel apprehensive, and even either sad or angry, when people or things change and we are not ready for it. In a healthy relationship, change and growth are allowed.

Take Care of You

You probably hope those around you like you, so you may try to please them. Don't forget to please yourself. Healthy relationships are mutual.

Be Dependable

If you make plans with someone, follow through with them. If you have an assignment deadline, meet it. If you take on a responsibility, complete it. Healthy relationships are trustworthy.

Fight Fair

Most relationships have some conflicts. It only means you disagree about something. Just because you disagree doesn't mean you don't like each other.

Negotiate a Time to Talk About It

Don't have difficult conversations when you are very angry or tired. Instead, ask when would be a good time to talk about something that is bothering you. Healthy relationships are based on respect, and respect must be reciprocal.

Don't Criticize

Attack the problem, not the person. Begin sensitive conversations with an "I" statement. Talk about how you struggle with the problem. Don't open with "You" statements. Avoid blaming the other person for your thoughts and feelings. Healthy relationships don't lay blame.

Don't Assign Feelings or Motives

Let others speak for themselves. Healthy relationships recognize each person's right to explain themselves.

Stay With the Topic

Don't use a current concern as a reason to jump into everything that bothers you. Healthy relationships don't use ammunition from the past to fuel the present. Say "I'm sorry" when you own it. That goes a long way towards making things right. Healthy relationships can admit mistakes.

Don't Assume Things

When we feel close to someone, it's easy to think we know how he or she feels. We can be very wrong. Healthy relationships check things out.

Don't Hold Grudges

You don't have to accept anything and everything, but don't hold grudges. Grudges just drain your energy. Studies show that the more we see the best in others, the better healthy relationships we will have. Healthy relationships don't hold on to past hurts and misunderstandings.

The Goal is for Everyone to be a Winner

Relationships with winners and losers don't last. Healthy relationships are between winners who seek answers to problems together.

You can Leave a Relationship

You can choose to move out of a relationship. Studies tell us that loyalty is very important in a relationship, and for the relationship to be healthy, it must have development, hope, and a future. These things are very important in a healthy relationship.

Show your Warmth

Study shows that warmth is highly valued by most people in their relationships. Healthy relationships show emotional warmth.

Keep your Life Balanced

Other people help make our lives satisfying, but they can't create that satisfaction for us. Only you can fill your life. Don't overload on activities, but do use your time wisely. Make sure that what you do is meaningful and desirable for you.

It's a Process

Sometimes it looks like everyone is confident and connected. Actually, most people feel just like you feel: wondering how to fit in and have a good relationship. It takes time to get to know other people, to make small talk, respond, and smile. Building healthy relationships is a process that can be learned and practiced, and it keeps getting better.

Be Yourself

It's so much easier and so much more fun to be you than to pretend to be something or someone else. Sooner or later, the pretense will catch up with you. Healthy relationships are made of real people, not images. Healthy relationships bring happiness to our lives. People with healthy relationships really do have more happiness and less stress.

CHAPTER 7

Keeping a Relationship Healthy

Relationships add richness and meaning to life. Friends, and networks of people, are valuable sources of enjoyment and support during difficult times. However, relationships must be maintained. It's easy to think that a loved one will always be there regardless of the situation, but it is also true that nobody likes to be taken for granted. Learn to keep a relationship healthy by following a few simple steps and using common sense.

Step 1 – Schedule Me In

Schedule in time for relationships. Time is one of the most important things people can give to their relationships. Work, school, children, and even hobbies can be time consuming. Inviting the person you share a relationship with to spend even an hour together with you has a positive and lasting impact. Spend time with those that time is worth spending with. Wasted time can never be gotten back [M.D. Neal]!

Step 2 – Support

Remember that support goes both ways. It is very important to keep things in a 50/50 balance. When a relationship partner is a good listener, it's easy to keep talking and forget that they may have problems too. Take time to ask your relationship partner how they are doing. Let them know you are interested in hearing about what is going on in their life.

Step 3 – Establish Boundaries

Establish boundaries and respect so you don't do anything that makes you uncomfortable, because this can compromise the relationship. Establishing boundaries helps to avoid resentment, anger, and communication problems. There is a time-tested saying that is still true today: TREAT OTHERS THE WAY YOU WANT TO BE TREATED.

Step 4 – Agree to Disagree

The person you're in a relationship with may not always see eye to eye with you, but, regardless of the outcome, handle disagreements with respect. Let your partner know that even if you think they are wrong about a topic you still care about them. Balance can be a determining factor: you can't always have your way. It is ok to disagree, because that is a part of life—but do not become disagreeable. The ability to disagree without being disagreeable is a sign of maturity.

Romans 12:17-18

Do not hit back, discover beauty in everything. If you've got it in you, get along with everybody. Don't insist on getting even. That's not for you to do.

Step 5 – Avoid Unhealthy Competition

Playing a game or any other activity together, or making a bet, can be engaging, but when winning becomes a priority, relationships get strained. Remember that your partner wants to have fun with you, not face a competition.

How to Tell If
The Relationship Is Unhealthy

Unhealthy —"harmful, mental stress; unwholesome; contributes to health issues"

During their teenage years, people start to form the kind of close relationships that are essential to the development of good mental health and happiness. If a relationship is healthy, you feel good around that person. You trust and respect them, and they feel accepted for who they are. However, because people are not perfect, most relationships are not totally healthy. If you recognize that a certain relationship has more bad elements than good, you should end the unhealthy relationship.

Step 1 – Language

Ask yourself if your partner frequently uses put-downs when they are talking to you. Imagine sharing a cherished memory or a secret with your partner and try to guess how they would respond. If most of what you imagine is hurtful, then the relationship is unhealthy. Although everyone has bad days every now and then, if most of what your partner says is hurtful, you should question the healthiness of that relationship. Partners should try to encourage and support each other. If your partner takes every opportunity to put you down, they are not a good partner.

Sticks and stones may break my bones but words will never hurt me? Not true: words can and will hurt if they are not used right. Being careful of what we say should always be taken into consideration.

Psalms 141:3

Post a guard at my mouth, God. Set a watch at the door of my lips.

Step 2 – Truthful or Not

Listen for lies. Good partners do no lie to each other. Even if the truth is hard to hear. If you catch your partner frequently lying, you cannot trust them. Find a new partner that is more trustworthy.

Colossians 3:9

Don't lie one to another. You're done with that old life. It's like a filthy set of ill-fitting clothes you've stripped off and put in the fire.

Step 3 – Pay Attention

Pay attention to your feelings. A relationship is unhealthy if the other person causes you to feel anger, hurt, or fear, more often than not. Many people mistake enemies for partners. If the basis of a relationship is jealousy, cheating, or greed, you will not feel good about yourself when you are with that person.

Step 4 – Take Notice

Notice the kinds of activities you do with your partner. Ask yourself if you are building your lives around healthy or unhealthy interests. If you spend most of the time eating junk food, drinking, smoking, doing drugs, or complaining, the relationship is unhealthy. A good relationship should make you want to be a better person, not serve as an excuse for your bad habits.

I Corinthians 15:33

Bad company ruins good manners.

Manners – "a way of acting, bearing, or behavior"

A good relationship would never put you at risk of not doing what is right, or tempt you to do what is wrong.

Step 5 – Give and Take

Ask yourself how much give and take is involved in your relationship. If you are giving 80% and your friend is giving 20%, the relationship is unhealthy. An unhealthy relationship involves a 50-50 split in give and take. If you are constantly giving more than you are receiving, consider ending the relationship.

Proverbs 10:9

Honesty lives confident and carefree, but shifty is sure to be exposed.

Be sure that this area is always taken seriously and fairly before you go too far, give too much, and end up with the short end of the stick.

Step 6 – Ponder This

Watch how you resolve conflict with your partner. If one person bullies the other, or if the partner becomes abusive, the relationship is unhealthy. All partners will disagree from time to time but in a healthy relationship partners respect each other and forgive each other. There should be a willingness to compromise and both partners should feel good about the way problems are solved.

CHAPTER 8

What You Say Does Matter

It is always easy to point the finger when you don't want to change. But if you want to change, you will go through the necessary processes that will help bring about development. Being able to understand what's important in life will always be the centerpiece that makes or breaks a relationship.

Matter deals with physical substance, mind, and spirit. A lot of times in a relationship we can say things that really don't matter, serve no point, and carry no weight. You say it because you can, in many cases, just wanting to hear yourself talk, or feeling the need to get your point across.

Sometimes, when you think back about an argument, you realize that what you were fighting about was actually trivial and pointless. It only flared up because you didn't take the time to deal with the "stuff in the basement," the little things, and by the time you made it to the first floor the issue was magnified, made bigger than it should have been. You never want to get to the point where you let trivial things escalate, preventing you from moving forward. This will affect the growth of the relationship every time. Allowing sensitive issues to lie dormant will eventually pull you down to a place you don't want to be.

What you say matters in three areas:

The Physical – how a person looks

The Mental – how a person thinks

The Spirit – how a person feels

What comes out of your mouth has the ability to help a person or hurt a person. Every relationship improves when the right things are said. Being able to select your words appropriately, according to the situation, is definitely a sign of maturity, because we so often say the right thing at the wrong time, or the wrong thing at the right time. Both are possible and damage relationships. Helpful words consist of five things:

W – Worth

O – Order

R – Restoration

D – Direction

S – Substance

Mark 11:20-21 – The fig tree dries up

While Jesus and His disciples were walking early in the morning they saw that the fig tree had dried up. Peter remembered what Jesus had said so he said to Jesus, Rabbi, look, the fig tree you cursed had dried up.

Jesus destroyed this fig tree from the roots so it could never form itself again. One of the worst things you can allow in a relationship is letting things form that are not productive. When this happens, it is an indication that the relationship will never provide what you need. This needs to be dealt with at the root, ASAP. In this particular chapter, Jesus' words carried out that order. He dealt with the root of this fig tree, so he would never have this problem out of this tree again. You will always find yourself dealing with the same problems if you try handling them from the surface alone. Sensitive issues need to be put in their proper place. Whenever you allow these to keep being a part of your relationships, you disqualify yourself as a candidate for having new chances in your life.

Remember this: anyone who cannot be productive with the things in their life will never be productive with you or your desires. Jesus' irritation with this fig tree was that it was no good for him because it had not produced any figs. There are three reasons why a fig tree would not produce fruit:

Because of its age

Because of too much nitrogen

Because of watering conditions

Fig tree not producing fruit because of its age:

The most common reason for a fig tree not to produce fruit is simply its age. Trees, like animals, need to reach a certain maturity before they can produce offspring.

This is absolutely amazing, and so true in any relationship. You have to be sure that the person you are dealing with has reached an age where they are able to produce a level of maturity.

One of the greatest problems we have in a relationship is trying to get somewhere or build something with an immature person who has not reached a place of growth that can be beneficial to the relationship—whether this is emotionally, physically, or financially. Being on two different maturity levels will create two different paths that will eventually lead to one major problem. You can never reach the same destination by going in two different directions in a relationship. Both partners must be on the same page and understand what the plan is and how they are going to go about achieving it. If this cannot be done with a person who is not mature enough, that person will never understand the process or the importance of being able to produce.

Fig tree not producing because of too much nitrogen:

Another common reason that a fig tree does not produce fruit is because of too much nitrogen. This commonly happens when you are using a fertilizer that is too high in nitrogen. What is fertilizer? It is a substance that increases capacity for growth.

Ok, sit up and really pay attention, because this is important and could just save you a whole lot of time, heartache, and misery. You don't ever want to get to the point where you are giving too much of your time, energy, and resources to support a relationship, and getting nothing in return. You should never lower yourself for a person who can't appreciate the investment that you have made—who is unable to grow for the sake of the relationship.

A relationship that reflects great potential and is heading in the direction of longevity is a well-balanced relationship. Let me say it again, an imbalanced relationship is like a car that has lost its balance and is in need of a front end alignment. It starts to pull to one side and will eventually start to eat up the tires and cause damage to them. It's no different in a relationship that has lost its balance. It pulls more on one person, and will soon cause that person to be eaten up. Health, money, time, energy, and feelings that are overwhelmed will lead to much more damage. You want to be sure that the relationship you are in is, and stays, well-balanced. It can be difficult, but you must avoid doing too much—trying to get a person to grow can cause you to become a crutch to them, enabling their weaknesses while failing to support your own desires.

Fig tree not producing because of watering conditions:

If a fig tree is suffering from water stress, caused by either too little or too much water, this can cause it to stop producing fruit or never to begin producing fruit at all.

This happens especially if it is a young tree. Water stress will send the tree into a survival mode, and it will simply not have the energy to be productive. You want to do whatever you can at all times. If your relationship is suffering from a stressful environment, it will never move forward.

Nothing is perfect, and every relationship has its challenges, but you need to be willing to do your part. The right amount of water is vital: not too little and not too much. You never want your partner to feel like you are not giving enough or not giving at all, or, on the other hand, that what you are giving has become pointless and is not needed at all. In either case, things will become stressful and nonproductive.

Giving what is needed for productivity will only come back to benefit you in the long run. You would have built a long-lasting relationship with a partner who has what you need and can give you what you want, to your complete satisfaction. Your investment is the key to your enjoyment. Remember two things: 1) you can't get mad at what you are getting, if you are not doing your part to maintain it; and 2) you can't get mad if someone else is enjoying what you never took the time to invest in.

CHAPTER 9

Your Relationship Can Be Improved

Do you sometimes feel like your relationship isn't quite what it used to be, and you really don't know where to start on repairing the damaged areas to help revive it? There are some powerful and proven ways to improve virtually any relationship. These tips also happen to be the key ingredients that go into making a good relationship work. So, even if you think everything is great, you can use this as a diagnostic tool to make sure you and your partner are on the same road to relationship bliss.

TIP 1 – Accept the Unsolvable

Unfortunately, according to Relationship Scientist, John Gottman, 69% of relationship conflicts are persistent problems. This means that they revolve around issues that tend to resurface no matter how long you've been together. If you find a problem seems to bring up painful emotions, you're looking at one that's persistent.

To keep this problem from ruining your relationship, you'll need to address the bigger issues underlying your difficulties. Take turns discussing with your partner what this loaded issue really means to you. When your partner is talking, your job is to listen, be non-judgmental, and find something in her/his perspective that makes sense to you. When it's your turn to talk she/he should be doing the same thing, by treading more gently into touchy areas. You should at least be able to agree to disagree or make some small concessions for one another.

TIP 2 – Focusing on What's Fixable

This is so important to keeping an argument from becoming an emotional roller coaster. Consider it fixable. One major area that causes tension in a relationship is finances.

In a longitudinal study by Economist, Jay Zagorsky, it was found that 33% of couples have seriously divergent views on income, wealth, and debt. In particular, the initial stages of living together may be especially fraught with monetary concerns. To keep this problem from spiraling out of control, sit down with your other half and craft a detailed action plan. Consult any resources that might help to get your finances on track. You should both be able to live with the new arrangement or it won't work. To get a good grip on financial matters, I believe that whoever is the more mature and disciplined in making good financial decisions should handle the money. I had developed bad habits growing up, and those habits spilled over into my marriage and caused my family to suffer. For years, I put my relationship with my wife in jeopardy because of the bad financial decisions I was making. I was destroying our family, so I had to put my pride aside and do what was best to save my family and my marriage. My marriage was fixable because I was fixable. Use this method to address any other problems in your life that you deem fixable.

TIP 3 – Breaking Negative Cycles

I had to work so hard in the financial area of my relationship because I was the kind of person who would withdraw and shut down when I was faced with something difficult. I would go for days without talking, not wanting to be bothered. I had to fight hard to overcome this because doing so would be key to our survival, especially when we found ourselves homeless.

Troubled relationships tend to follow certain patterns. In a withdrawal pattern, one person tends to be more critical and demanding, while the other tends to withdraw or shut down in response to conflict. Douglas Tilley, a proponent of emotion-focused therapy, notes that 85% of the time, when men follow a withdrawal pattern, the reason may be biological. Men's cardiovascular systems are more responsive to stress, so tuning out your mate is an attempt to avoid an uncomfortable physical condition.

You can break negative patterns in your relationship. The next time things get heated, let your partner know what's going on with you by saying, "I can see the issue is important to you. I'm feeling too angry to discuss it right now, so let's come back to it once I have cooled off." Coming back to deal with something at a later time is often the best way to avoid mishandling it in the heat of the moment. (Note: If you are going to win, you will have to acknowledge your limitations).

TIP 4 – Understand Anger

This is a very sensitive and important part of being able to cope and survive within a relationship. For the nearly two-year stretch when my family was homeless, I knew I had to develop a comfortable environment for me, my wife and our kids, if our marriage had any chance of making it. It's hard, and can be impossible, to overcome any difficulty if you are not comfortable.

Living in a Super 8 Hotel that cost us $50 per night was indeed an experience in itself. One room was infested with ants, another room was mildewed, and in another room the ceiling fell in while I was getting ready to step into the shower. Nights that I could not afford a room, we had to make our beds in my 1998 Ford Expedition truck while living out of green trash bags. What helped me to keep down the anger was knowing that I was doing the best I could. As crazy as it may sound, I was doing the best I could to make the environment comfortable. I must admit, this was one of the best times of our lives, and it drew the whole family closer in a way we never could have imagined.

While outbursts of anger are common even in healthy relationships, when anger becomes an entrenched part of a couple's life, it is cause for concern. Johnson Master is a therapist and a pioneer of emotions-focused therapy Emotions-focused therapy is an empirically validated treatment for distressed relationships. It refers to anger as a secondary emotion that fronts for primary emotions such as sadness or a fear of being abandoned. Think back to the last argument you had with your partner and use this new knowledge to look for hidden messages in what each of you was trying to communicate. Try to disregard the angry tones you both used and try to tune in to what you were really trying to say. This will help you to see that you both have needs that makes sense. For instance, "You are a workaholic!" might really mean, "I miss you and want to spend more time with you." Being able to harness and control anger will always produce a comfortable and successful environment.

TIP 5 – Find Common Goals

A study in collaboration with a dating site in the UK found that 13% of couples reported no longer having the same goals. This situation represents a ticking time bomb. As research has shown, couples who share dreams and goals have long-lasting, more satisfying relationships. If you feel like you have been out of sync lately with your partner on this front, discuss your philosophy of life together. The aim is for both of you to share what you want your life to be about, where you want to end up, and what these things mean to you. Look for anything that's common between the two of you, and talk about ways to work towards that aspiration together.

TIP 6 – Share Power

When a man is not willing to share his power with his relationship partner, John Gottman's research indicates that there is an 81% chance that this relationship will self-destruct. While hoarding power may have gotten you ahead in your career, this strategy will backfire in your relationship, because your wife/husband will end up feeling like her/his opinions are not valuable and don't matter to you. To help save your relationship, you must develop a more accepting attitude towards compromise. Practice by giving in on issues you don't feel extremely invested in.

TIP 7 – Don't Distort

Researchers have known for a long time that unhappy couples focus on the negatives in their relationships. An early study by Robinson and Price in 1980 found that unhappy couples underestimate the occurrence of pleasurable events in their relationships by 50%. Relatedly, Fincham, Beach and Baucom found in 1987 that individuals in distressed relationships were prone to attributing negative intentions to their partners' behavior. If you find yourself stuck in this rut of distorted thinking, the next time you have a negative thought about something your partner has done, try to come up with a more neutral explanation for his/her actions. Another strategy is to consider whether you would judge yourself so harshly if the situation were reversed. Finally, remind yourself often of the good times you have spent together recently.

TIP 8 – Concentrate on the Present to Ensure Your Future

Interestingly, the ability of your relationship to weather tough times has a lot to do with your mutual availability in the here and now. Unfortunately, over time and for a variety of reasons, many couples move further apart from each other. This means that when a rough patch hits, their relationship doesn't survive.

To build a rock-solid relationship, start by acknowledging rather than ignoring the ordinary moments in your relationship. If your partner wants to share something she/he is reading on the internet, for example, take a minute to listen even if you simply grunt in response. It may sound strange, but if you accumulate enough of these little things, when you really need your partner they will be there for you.

TIP 9 – Appreciate Each Other

Remember when you first started dating how you used to go that extra mile to impress her or him. Well, one of the secrets to a long and fulfilling relationship is to continue to actively appreciate your partner. You don't necessarily have to pull out all the stops the way you did back in the day, but regular efforts to show your partner that you appreciate them will do wonders for keeping your relationship strong.

If you are not sure where to start, a good place is by doling out daily compliments. Tell her/him how good they look, or thank them for some kind of abilities they have. The only rule to this is to make sure you genuinely mean what you say.

TIP 10 – Solidify Your Relationship

How satisfied you feel in your relationship has a lot to do with how connected you feel to your partner. Research suggests that our ability to connect with others (our attachment style) is influenced by our childhood experiences. According to Prior and Glasser's 2006 research, 65% of children can be classified as having a secure attachment style, while the remaining 35% having an insecure attachment style.

As an adult, an insecure attachment style is associated with a slew of relationship troubles, including jealously, obsession, and emotional highs and lows. The good news is that regardless of your present pattern you can become more securely attached or connected to your partner by developing a deeper relationship. To do that, incrementally spend more time with each other doing something you both enjoy. Also, regularly ask for updates on your partner's likes and dislikes, current stressors, and new interests, because everyone changes over time.

CHAPTER 10

Love Is a Lifestyle, Not a Language

Love Is What You Do, Not What You Say!!

This chapter contains excerpts taken from the concepts I taught in my G.R.O.W.T.H. Empowerment Class. Love is an action word. You don't have to say that you love me, although it's nice to hear, but I would prefer that you show me. Show me by the way you look at me, the way you hold me, the way that you touch me. Let me know that you care by listening to me, even when you don't want to.

I guess I had to learn that loves goes so much deeper than what I was taught. And, I had to learn that love can be given and received in different ways. No two people will ever love the same and no two people will receive or give love the same. Love is a learned behavior. This is why it's vital that the right person teaches you about love and how to love.

When I first started dating my wife, because of her past hurts, she didn't believe me when I would tell her that I loved her. She had been told this time and time again, only to be hurt and disappointed. So, I knew that I had to take a different approach and literally show her that I loved her. Words didn't mean anything to this woman. It was almost as if she would look right through me when I uttered those three words. Have you ever had the feeling that you were talking to someone and they were looking right at you but didn't hear a word you said? Yup, that was the look she would give me! I figured out that I would have to show her, so that's what I did, and in doing this I was able to break down, slowly, the fortress of walls that she had around her heart. I could always tell when I had a small victory because she would always say, "You sure think you're slick." That was her way of saying, "I'm letting you in, but you still have a long way to go." I had to show her that I loved her by accepting her faults, her anger, and by being there for her for the countless nights that she cried.

There is nothing worse than having someone cry and not being able to do anything about it except hold them and try to hold it together yourself. Love can be the most joyous thing you ever experience, but it can also be the most painful thing that you ever experience. Showing her that I loved her developed into learning how to show others how to love, in spite of the person or the things that the person may have done. So, hopefully, this chapter will help you to understand how to show love. And then perhaps you too will decide to teach others what you have learned.

LESSON 1 – 5/28/2014

L.O.V.E.

L – Loyal – To be faithful to

O – Observing – Direct attention

V – Vibrant – Energy

E – Everlasting – Without limits

Love is not a noun—it is a verb, an action word. Love will serve as the bridge to support the breakdowns in your life. Love will get you from bad times to better times. The author of the following quote is unknown, but they said, "Love is a symbol of eternity – it wipes out all sense of time, destroying all memory of a beginning and all fear of an end…"

In other words, love is always creating the moment. The reason why some of us hit a place where we struggle with our love is because we start looking back at how it all started, which causes us to become frustrated with what it has become, and how it might end up. This could possibly destroy where you are now.

Somewhere in there, you stopped loving in the moment, and allowed the moment to determine how you would love.

3 POINTS

Point 1 – Love is understanding the process.

Process – "a series of actions, changes, or functions bringing about a result"

Romans 5:6-8

V.6 – *Look at it this way, at the right time, while we were still helpless, Christ died for ungodly people.*

V.7 – *Finding someone who would die for a godly person is rare, maybe someone would have the courage to die for a good person.*

V.8 – *Christ died for us while we were still sinners and demonstrates God's love for us.*

Maybe you need to die to yourself to give that person the chance to live through their mess.

Back-up scripture – Ephesians 4:2-3

V.2 – *Be humble and gentle in every way; be patient with*

each other and lovingly accept each other.

V.3 – *Through the peace that ties you together, do your best to maintain the unity that the spirit gives.*

Point 2 – Love Will Never Entangle Itself with Motives

Motive – "The reason for a certain course of action, whether conscious or unconscious"

I Peter 1:22

V.22 – Love each other with a warm love that comes from the heart; after all, you have purified yourselves by obeying the truth, as a result you have a sincere love for each other.

What cleanses you from any impurities to be able to love right if obeying what the word tells you to do.

Back-up scripture – Jeremiah 3:14

V.14 – Come back, you rebellious people, declares the Lord. I am your husband, I will take you one from every city and two from every family and bring you Zion.

God makes a commitment to those who are doing wrong, and yet also makes them a promise; in other words, He is saying, my love is strong enough to get you right, if you let it.

POINT 3 – Love has to be stronger than your emotions.

Emotion – "a strong agitation of feelings caused by experiencing something"

You can never allow your love to be controlled by what you have experienced, or been through.

Matthew 5:43-48

V.43 – You have heard that it was said, love your neighbor and hate your enemy.

V.44 – But I tell you this, love your enemies and pray for those who persecute you.

V.45 – In this way you show that you are children of your Father in Heaven. He makes his sun rise on people whether they are good or evil. He lets rain fall on them whether they are just or unjust.

V.46 – If you love those who love you do you deserve a reward? Even the tax collectors do that.

V.47 – *Are you doing anything remarkable if you welcome only your friends, everyone does that?*

V.48 – *That is why you must be perfect, as your Father in Heaven is perfect.*

Love can never be directed by emotions, because emotions will always direct love wrong.

LESSON 2 – 6/11/2014

James Baldwin once said, "Love does not begin and end the way we seem to think it does. Love is a battle, love is a war, love is growing." In other words, love requires effort and it can't be immature. Love has to be worked on and worked at if you want to see the results you desire. Operating in a sense of immaturity will always cause some type of misunderstanding and conflict. In order for love to last, its conduct has to always be considered when you're dealing in a level of maturity.

3 POINTS

POINT 1 – Love can be affected by influence.

Influence – "The power to sway or affect based on prestige (how powerful you are), wealth (how much money you have), ability (what you can do), or position (how close you are)'

Must Read – Matthew 24:4-12

POINT 2 – Love cannot survive off a percentage – it has to be all or nothing.

Luke 10:27

V.27 – *He answered. Love the Lord your God with all your heart, with all your soul, with all your strength, and with all your mind, and love your neighbor as you love yourself.*

There are four things love has to be in order for it to function:

1 – Passionate

2 – Spiritual

3 – Strong

4 – Mentally Involved

POINT 3 – Love can't take on the appearance of a mannequin – you dress it up but it ain't real.

In other words, it can't be fake; looking good on the outside but with no ability to move.

Must Read – Romans 12:9-19

When you know who you are you don't allow the ignorance of other people to cause you to stoop down to their level.

LESSON 3 – 6/14/2014

Hosea 4:6 says – *My people are destroyed because of the lack of knowledge.*

When you know better, you should do better. Sometimes you can mistake what you see being done as love.

Understanding love has to be taught—the importance and structure of it. Barbara De Angelis once said, "Love is a force more formidable than any other. It is visible. It cannot be seen or measured, yet it is powerful enough to transform you in a moment and offer you more joy than any material possession could. In other words, love has the ability to change you and make you happy. Love is always bigger than stuff."

3 POINTS

POINT 1 – Love is fulfilling.

Fulfilling –"to satisfy, to make complete"

Love can never be empty. It should never feel like something is missing.

Must Read – Romans 8-10

So, love has to be taught!

Adultery – "desiring what doesn't belong to you"

Love is not down with O.P.P.: Other People's Property.

Murder – "depriving of life"

Steal – "to take from"

Bearing False Witness – "believing everything it hears"

Covet – "understands where it is and does not create added pressure – it's satisfied"

Covet (2) – "to wish, long, or crave for something (especially the property of another person)"

David said, "*When I saw the prosperity of the wicked my foot almost slipped.*"

POINT 2 – Love is greater than your abilities and a reflection of your humility.

Abilities – "what you can do or what you are good at"

Humility – "a personal worth – it's what you are made of"

Must Read – I Corinthians 13:1-8

Part 1 – Your Abilities (I Corinthians 13:1-3)

Part 2 – Your Humility (I Corinthians 13:4-8)

All these things will come to an end but love never ends

POINT 3 – Love does not openly expose

Expose – to deprive of shelter or protection – lay open to danger or harm

There is a difference in seeking wise counsel to help your situation or condition versus you just throwing somebody under the bus or airing out their dirty laundry.

Must Read – I Peter 4:7-11

You can't properly love without having God in your life. God gets glory when we demonstrate love. I John 4:8 (NIV) says – whoever does not love, does not know God, because God is love.

LESSON 4 – 8/3/2014

Immature love says I love you because I need you. Mature love says I need you because I love you.

Immature – "not fully grown or developed – a lack of wisdom, insight, and emotional stability"

Mature – "full development – mental or physical"

3 POINTS

POINT 1 – Love knows when saying nothing is best.

Isaiah 53:7 – *He was oppressed and he was afflicted yet he opened not his mouth, He was led as a lamb to the slaughter as a sheep before its shearers is silent so he opened not His mouth.*

POINT 2 – Love will do what's best before it makes a mess.

Matthew 1:18-20

V.18 – *Now the birth of Jesus Christ was as follows; after his mother Mary was betrothed to Joseph before they came together she was found with child of the Holy Spirit.*

Any crisis must be carefully thought out.

Crisis – A sudden change in the course, an unstable condition, a turning point

V.19 – *Then Joseph her husband, being a just man and not wanting to make her a public example, was minded to put her away secretly.*

Joseph was a just man. Before you do anything make sure you are all the way right first. Not wanting to make her a public example is a perfect example of love that will never expose what it is committed to.

Expose – "to deprive of shelter (cover) or protection, lay open to danger or harm"

Proverbs 10:12 (NLT) – *Hatred stirs up quarrels (fight) but love makes up for all offenses (wrong doing).*

I Peter 4:8 (NLT) – *Most important of all, continue to show deep love for each other, for love covers a multitude of sins.*

Deep – "extending far downward below a surface"

Real love will always be willing to go deep to prevent destruction (I'm in too deep). Some of y'all are suffering because you are trying to survive off of surface love.

Surface – "a portion of space having length and breadth but no thickness"

There is too much space between you all, which is causing things to thin out. It's not as thick as it use to be. There is an old saying, which says, we are thick as thieves. But are you really?

Matthew 1:20 – *But while he thought about these things, behold, an angel of the Lord appeared to him in a dream saying, Joseph son of David, do not be afraid to take to you*

Mary, your wife, for that which is conceived in her is of the
Holy Spirit.

Appearance is the key when you are trying to sort things out. Who you are seen with is very important. You can't be seen with the wrong sorts, or people will instantly think you are just like them. The Lord came to him in a dream when he had control over his actions. You have to be very careful of people coming to you when you have lost control of what's going on.

That which was conceived in her was of the Holy Spirit, but what have you allowed to be conceived in you?

> **Conceived** – "to form or hold or develop in the mind; to become pregnant with"

POINT 3 – Love will give what it has to keep what it's got.

V.10 – So he arose and went to Zare-Phath, and when he came to the gate of the city indeed a widow was there gathering sticks, and he called to her and said, please bring me a little water in a cup that I may drink.

Your potential is connected to your prophet. Everything that you need is in the mouth of the prophet.

Potential – "capable of being but not yet in existence"

You can't allow your condition to cause you to be critical.

Matthew 10:41 (NLT) – *If you receive a prophet as on who speaks for God you will be given the same reward as a prophet.*

V.11 – And as she was going to get it he called to her and said please bring me a morsel of bread in your hand.

How a person responds to your test will determine your

turnaround. It's all about having the right people around you at the right time.

> V.12 – *So she said as the Lord your God lives, I do not have bread, only a handful of flour in a bin and a little oil in a jar, and see, I am gathering a couple of sticks that I may go in and prepare it for myself and my son that we may eat it and die.*

You have to be able to identify what you have in order to be able to know how far it will go.

> V.13 – *And Elijah said to her, do not fear. Go and do as you have said but make me a small cake from it first. and bring it to me, and afterwards make some for yourself and your son.*

> V.14 – *For thus says the Lord God of Israel, the bin of flour shall not be used up, nor shall the jar of oil run dry until the day of the Lord send rain on earth.*

Your obedience is important to your outcome. Obedience will carry you further than you could ever imagine, but you must keep your mind stayed on God during the process.

Hebrews 13:17 (NIV) – *Have confidence in your leaders and submit to their authority because they keep watch over you as those who must give an account. Do this so that their work will be a joy, not a burden, for that would be of no benefit to you. Make me a small cake from it first, then go make one for you and your son is what she was told. Don't let what you see make you miss what you hear. You must have keen ears in this season to hear exactly what the Lord is saying so that you don't miss out what He wants to give to you and do for you.*

V.15 – So she went away and did according to the word of Elijah and she and he and her household ate for many days.

What you do will affect those who are connected to you. When she was facing death they only mentioned her and her son but when she followed the words of the man of God, they mentioned a household. It is imperative that you think about how everyone will be affected by your decisions because love will give what it has to keep what it has. She loved her son indeed.

Tips that will help you better your love:

1 – Decide what you want out of it.

2 – Have something to offer the other person.

3 – Get involved with people (don't always keep to yourself).

4 – Give it time (don't force things).

5 – Commit (you have to put effort into it)

6 – Learn lessons and apply them when moving forward.

7 – Work constantly on making yourself better.

8 – Eliminate jealously.

9 – Try to see issues from all sides.

10 – Don't expect perfection.

This book was designed to make your journey throughout life a successful one. As you continuously revisit the chapters, follow the guidelines that are given. So that not only you but those around you will grow and your journey on the "SHIPS" will be triumphant.

Contact

For bookings/scheduling/inquiries:

Marques D. Neal Ministries

P.O. Box 1098

Brandywine, MD 20613

Email – mdnminitries@gmail.com

Voice – 571-620-2907

References

Averill, F. (2013, February 1). The 10 Proven Ways to Improve Your Relationship.

Retrieved September 18, 2014 from:

http://www.innovativefinancial.com/newsletters/February 2013/lg.html.

Plato, B. (2011). *Plato's the republic.* Place of publication not identified: Nmd Books.

Tarrant, J. (2008). *Bring Me the Rhinoceros: And Other Zen Koans That Will Save Your Life* (Second Ed.) Boston: Shambhala Publications.

All definitions taken from www.dictionary.com.

Made in the USA
Middletown, DE
25 June 2016